MW01538740

How to Pray Salah for Women and Girls

A Step-By-Step Guide to Connecting with Your Creator Through Islamic Prayer

© **Copyright 2024 - All rights reserved.**

The content contained within this book may not be reproduced, duplicated, or transmitted without direct written permission from the author or the publisher.

Under no circumstances will any blame or legal responsibility be held against the publisher or author for any damages, reparation, or monetary loss due to the information contained within this book, either directly or indirectly.

Legal Notice:

This book is copyright-protected. It is only for personal use. You cannot amend, distribute, sell, use, quote, or paraphrase any part of the content within this book without the consent of the author or publisher.

Disclaimer Notice:

Please note the information contained within this document is for educational and entertainment purposes only. All effort has been executed to present accurate, up-to-date, reliable, and complete information. No warranties of any kind are declared or implied. Readers acknowledge that the author is not engaging in the rendering of legal, financial, medical, or professional advice. The content within this book has been derived from various sources. Please consult a licensed professional before attempting any techniques outlined in this book.

By reading this document, the reader agrees that under no circumstances is the author responsible for any losses, direct or indirect, that are incurred as a result of the use of the information contained within this document, including, but not limited to, errors, omissions, or inaccuracies.

Table of Contents

Introduction

Allah (SWT) calls on you five times a day. Many Muslims rush to mosques or praying mats to answer the blessed call. Performing salah is every Muslim's duty, but it is more than a religious ritual. It is a spiritual worship act that purifies your heart, allows you to communicate with Allah (SWT), and deepens your connection. Salah is the Almighty's (SWT) gift to Muslims to protect them from bad deeds and sinning.

The book begins by explaining the importance of salah in Islam and how it brings you close to Allah (SWT). You will find tips on how girls and women can perform salah correctly and how it can strengthen your relationship with Allah (SWT).

Before practicing salah, Muslims should familiarize themselves with the five daily prayers. You will learn about each salah, its time, and number of rak'ahs. Setting intentions is a big part of worship. You will discover the significance of niyyah, sincerity in salah, and the words to recite before praying,

Allah (SWT) commanded five prayers a day for a reason. You will learn about their history, significance, and benefits.

Salah requires physical, mental, and spiritual preparation. Discover how to perform wudu with a step-by-step guide. Learn about the significance of cleanliness and modesty in preparation for salah.

It is easy to get distracted when praying, so you should assign a quiet place at home to focus while worshiping Allah (SWT). Learn how to create a peaceful environment to help you focus when you pray at home.

After preparing for salah, you should understand how to pray as the Prophet Muhammed (PUH) taught his companions. The book provides a beginner-friendly guide with detailed instructions on the physical movements of salah and what to say in each one. You will learn what to do in each rak'ah and how to recite Al-Fatiha.

You will be guided to learn how to focus and concentrate during salah and eliminate distractions.

Some Muslims only pray in their free time and fail to prioritize this significant worship act. You will find tips on how to maintain a consistent prayer practice.

You will also learn about the differences in prayer postures between men and women, and have insight about menstruation and postnatal rules for worship. The book also provides supplications for women's different needs.

Improve your prayer experience and learn about the importance of consistency and how to improve your devotion in salah.

A few misconceptions and challenges associated with salah affect your worship. You can find guidance on how to overcome them with helpful tips.

The book ends with a frequently asked questions section and resources to help you learn more about salah.

Begin your spiritual journey and discover the beauty of prayer!

Chapter 1: Everything You Should Know About Salah

Do you wish to be close to Allah (SWT)? Do you want to talk to Him whenever you feel sad, angry, or afraid? Muslims want to feel connected to Allah (SWT) and feel the peacefulness of Islam in their hearts. Some believe you can only get this feeling while performing Hajj and worshiping near the Kaaba. However, Allah (SWT) gave you a gift to remember Him, connect with Him, and recharge your heart with the power of Iman every day. It is the gift of salah.

1. Prayer brings you closer to Allah (SWT). Source: https://www.pexels.com/photo/person-kneeling-with-face-on-ground-7249372/

This chapter explains the significance of salah in Islam, how girls and women can perform salah correctly, how to deepen your connection with Allah (SWT) through prayer, and the importance of the concept of salah.

Importance of Salah in Islam

Salah is one of the five pillars of Islam and comes second after shahadah (profession of faith), reflecting its significance. Allah (SWT) sent many of his commands to Prophet Muhammed (PBUH) through the angel Jibreel (AS), except the salah. Allah (SWT) commanded it directly from His Prophet (PBUH) on a special occasion, the Isra' and Mi'raj. During the blessed Isra' and Mi'raj, Prophet Muhammed (PBUH) ascended to the heavens and met the holy prophets.

The word salah is mentioned in the Quran in over 60 verses and Allah (SWT) spoke about its importance.

"Indeed, prayer prohibits immorality and wrongdoing, and the remembrance of Allah is greater. And Allah knows that which you do." Quran 29:45.

Salah protects Muslims from sinning and committing vices that are against Islam's teachings. It also purifies the heart, protects it from temptation, materialism, moral decay, egoism, and worldly distractions, and provides guidance and reassurance to all worshipers. Salah also gives Muslims resilience and strength to overcome life's challenges. Allah (SWT) rewards believers who perform the five prayers on time and are dedicated to worship.

Salah gives you the chance to repent for your sins. By prostrating, you become closer to Allah (SWT) and can ask for His forgiveness and beg Him to purify your heart and mind from anything that could anger Him. Prophet Muhammed (PBUH) said in a hadith, *"A slave becomes nearest to his Rubb (God) when he is in prostration. So increase supplications while prostrating."*

Praying five times a day renews your commitment to Islam and gives you a sense of tranquility. Salah gives you refuge as you feel the presence of Allah (SWT) in your heart and around you. It teaches you discipline, compassion, humility, and gratitude.

How Girls and Women Can Perform Salah Correctly

- Women and girls cannot pray when they are on their menstrual cycle.

- Once the bleeding stops, cleanse yourself.

- Remove any filth such as blood, urine, feces, vomit, and pus from your body, clothes, prayer mat, and the place where you perform salah.

- To purify yourself, you should perform wudu or ablution before performing salah.

- Dress appropriately and cover your hair and whole body except for your face and hands.

- Place your prayer mat in the qiblah's direction.

- Stand on the mat and prepare yourself for praying.

- Your body should also face the qiblah.

- Set your intention or niyyah and start praying.

Deepen Your Connection with Allah Through Prayer

True happiness lies in being close to Allah (SWT) and connecting with Him on a deeper level. Salah deepens this connection. You stand before Allah (SWT) five times a day, talking to Him and submitting completely to Him. You recite the verses of the Quran and the words of the Almighty (SWT) and feel every word in your heart.

During prayer, you repeat *Allahu Akbar, Subḥāna rabbīl-ʿaẓīm, and Subḥāna rabbīl-ʿalā* which are an acknowledgment of Allah's (SWT) superiority. You are saying that Allah (SWT) is bigger, greater, and higher than everything and everyone. These words mean that Allah (SWT) is more powerful than your problems or pain. They are a reminder that Allah (SWT) is always there, and that you're never alone. No matter what happens, you know that He will never abandon you.

Muslims are closest to Allah (SWT) during prayer. This provides you with a unique opportunity to make dua, express your gratitude for all the blessings He gave you, ask for forgiveness, and pray for anything you want.

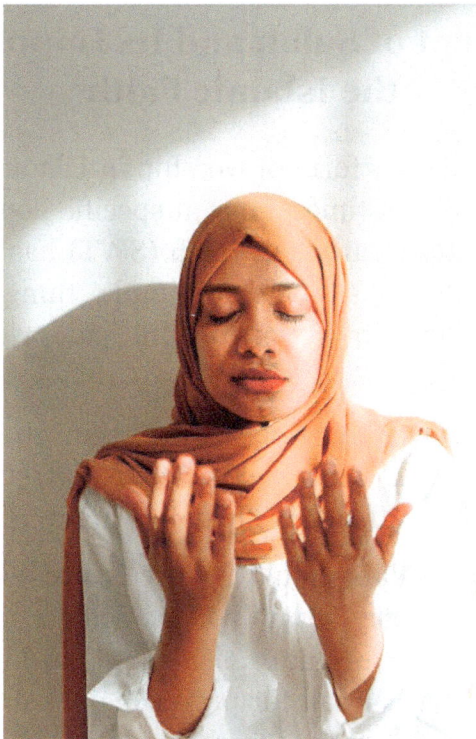

2.   Muslims are closest to Allah (SWT) during prayer. Source: https://www.pexels.com/photo/photo-of-a-woman-in-a-brown-hijab-praying-7956745/

Making dua while praying can deepen your connection with Allah (SWT). It allows you to directly communicate with Him and speak to Him in your own words, creating a deep spiritual connection with the Almighty (SWT).

When you make dua, you are only talking to Allah (SWT). No one can hear you but Him. The Merciful is listening to you with love and compassion without judgment. You are speaking to the only one who can solve your problems and ease your pain.

The Concept of Salah and Its Importance in the Islamic Faith

Salah is a mandatory form of worship in Islam. Muslims are required to pray five times a day at specific hours that differ from one country to another. Allah (SWT) has given you so much and only asks you for simple things in return. Performing salah allows you to fulfill your rights to Allah (SWT).

Praying involves reciting verses from the Quran and performing certain movements while surrendering your heart and mind to Allah (SWT), for you are in His presence.

Unlike Hajj, salah should be performed every day and multiple times a day, so it has become a part of every Muslim's life. Salah reunites all Muslims in one place. The moment the azhan or call for prayer ends, believers rush to the mosque. They all stand together side by side, the rich and poor, to worship Allah (SWT).

Salah is one of the most important acts of worship in Islam. Prophet Muhammed (PBUH) explained its significance in a hadith, *"On the Day of Judgment, a slave will be questioned about his prayers first. If his prayers are good, his other deeds will be good, too. If his prayers are bad, his other deeds will be bad, too."* It is also the dearest act of worship to Allah (SWT) and the most virtuous deed in Islam.

Salah isn't an obligation but a gift from Allah (SWT) to all Muslims. It brings you closer to Him and creates a deep connection that can make you happier and more fulfilled.

Chapter 2: The Five Daily Prayers Simplified

Muslims pray at dawn, before noon, in the afternoon, at sunset, and in the evening to worship Allah (SWT) at different times. As a result, they always feel connected to the Almighty (SWT) and can turn to Him whenever they need guidance. This chapter explains the five daily prayers, the importance of niyyah, and the significance of each prayer time and its benefits.

3.   Muslims pray 5 times a day. Source:
https://www.pexels.com/photo/woman-in-black-hijab-sitting-on-blue-and-brown-area-rug-7249336/

Overview of the Five Daily Prayers

A muezzin is the man who calls to prayer or adhan in the mosque. The adhan begins with the words *"Allahu Akbar"* repeated four times, meaning *"Allah is great,"* and they acknowledge Allah's (SWT) superiority. Then the muezzin repeats the shahadah or profession of faith twice, *"Ash-hadu alla ilaha illa-llah we Ash-hadu anna Muhammad-Rasulullah"* meaning *"I bear witness that there is no God but God and Prophet Muhammed (PBUH) is His messenger."*

The muezzin then says, *"Hayya 'ala-s-Salah"* and *"Hayya 'ala-l-falah,"* meaning, *"Come to prayer"* and *"Come to success."* He ends the adhan by saying *"Allahu Akbar"* twice and *"La ilaha illa-llah,"* meaning, *"There is no God but Allah (SWT)."*

Adhan is the same for all prayers except el fajr (the sunrise prayer) where, *"As-Salatu khairun min an-naum,"* meaning *"Prayer is better than sleep,"* is said after *"Hayya 'ala-s-falah."*

After the adhan comes the iqama, or standing up for prayer, which announces that salah at the mosque is about to start.

Fajr

This is the first salah of the day and takes place at dawn before sunrise. You pray two rak'ahs where you will recite Surah Al-Fatihah and any verses from the Quran. Recite the Quran loudly if you are praying alone, with other women, or with mahrams such as your father, brother, husband, or son. If non-mahrams or strange men are present, pray in a low voice. Fajr has two sunnah rak'ahs that you should pray first.

Sunnah prayers are the salah that Prophet Muhammed (PBUH) prayed with the five main prayers. They aren't obligatory but hold great rewards. It is forbidden to pray after the fajr until the sun rises.

Dhuhr

Dhuhr is the second prayer of the day and takes place before or right after noon. It consists of four rak'ahs that you pray in a low voice, even if you are praying alone. Pray two or four rak'ahs sunnah before the dhuhr and two after it.

Asr

Asr is the third prayer and takes place in the afternoon. It consists of four rak'ahs and no sunnah. Asr is performed in a low voice. It is forbidden to pray after the asr until the sun sets.

Maghrib

Maghrib is the fourth prayer and takes place after sunset. It consists of three rak'ahs. The first two are recited loudly, and the third one is recited in a low voice. Maghrib has two sunnah that are prayed after.

Isha

Isha is the fifth and last prayer of the day. It takes place in the evening and consists of four rak'ahs. The first two are recited loudly, and the last two are recited in a low voice. Isha has two sunnah rak'ahs that are prayed after.

The Value of Intention (Niyyah)

Niyyah is an Arabic word that means intention, and it is the motive behind your thoughts and actions. Muslims should set a niyyah before doing any good deed, including acts of worship. For instance, you lied to your boss and said you are sick and can't come to work. You feel guilty, so you ask Allah (SWT) to forgive you. You also pay sadaqah or charity with the intention that Allah (SWT) forgives you for lying.

Niyah is very important in salah as it distinguishes it from worldly acts. Prophet Muhammed (PBUH) said, *"The reward of deeds depends upon the intention, and every person will get the reward according to what he has intended."*

Niyyah goes beyond saying phrases you have memorized. It isn't a ritual that anyone should repeat mindlessly. It is when your heart, mind, and actions align with the purpose of salah. It is the act of deciding to devote yourself to Allah (SWT) and dedicating your energy and time to strengthening your relationship with Him and seeking His pleasure.

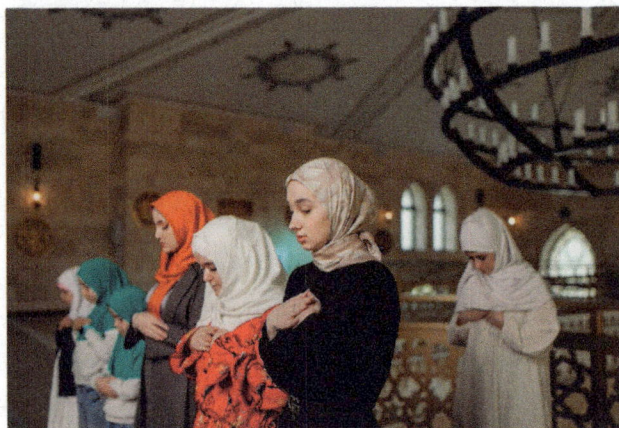

4. *You know your intentions are pure when the heart, mind, and actions align with the purpose of salah. Source: https://www.pexels.com/photo/women-praying-in-a-mosque-8164746/*

With these thoughts in mind, you should set niyyah to perform salah to be close to Allah (SWT), worship Him, and submit to His will. Your intentions should be pure, and your words should come from the heart to establish a spiritual connection with the Almighty (SWT). Set your niyyah before every prayer to surrender yourself to the Almighty (SWT).

The Importance of Sincerity in Salah

The Prophet Muhammed (PBUH) was sitting in Al Masjid al Nabawi when a man entered to offer salah. He prayed in a hurry with no sincerity. After he finished, the Prophet (PBUH) told him to go back and repeat his prayer. The man did. However, the Prophet (PBUH) still wasn't pleased with his prayer and told him to repeat it again. The man prayed again, but the Prophet made the same request.

The man realized that he was doing something wrong and asked the Prophet (PBUH) for guidance. Prophet Muhammed (PBUH) advised him to perform salah calmly, with dignity, and to give it all his attention.

Salah isn't a chore that one should perform mindlessly or quickly to get it over with. You should be sincere in your prayer and recognize that you are standing before Allah (SWT). Anything in the world can wait, but nothing should be more important than these few minutes you pray and connect with Allah (SWT).

The Words to be Recited

Repeat these words to set an intention before every salah:

Fajr

"I intend to pray two rak'ah Fard of Subh facing the qibla for Allah, the Great."

Dhuhr

"I intend to pray four rak'ah Fard of Dhuhar facing the qibla for Allah, the Great."

Asr

"I intend to pray four rak'at Fard of 'Asr facing the qibla for Allah, the Great."

Maghrib

"I intend to pray three rak'ah Fard of Maghrib facing the qibla for Allah, the Great."

Isha

"I intend to pray four rak'at Fard of 'Ishaa facing the qibla for Allah, the Great."

History and Significance of Each Prayer Time and Its Associated Benefits

Allah (SWT) commanded Prophet Muhammed (PBUH) when he ascended to the heavens that Muslims should pray 50 times a day. On his way down, the Prophet (PBUH) met Prophet Musa (AS), who told him that his followers wouldn't be able to handle it. Prophet Muhammed (PBUH) returned to Allah (SWT) and asked Him to reduce the number and Allah (SWT) reduced them to 45.

Prophet Musa (AS) said that it was still too much. Prophet Muhamed (PBUH) asked Allah (SWT) again for a reduction, and He made them 40 prayers. However, Prophet Musa (AS) again told him that it would be hard.

Prophet Muhammed (PBUH) kept returning to Allah (SWT) until they were reduced to five prayers.

Each of the five prayers is determined by the sun's position in the sky and your location. Prophet Muhammed (PBUH) said in a hadith that Jibreel (AS) prayed dhuhr with him at noon, then asr when everything had a shadow, maghrib when the sun set, and fasting Muslims were having their iftar, isha when the twilight was gone, and fajr at dawn when fasting people weren't allowed to eat. This was how Prophet Muhammed learned the time of each prayer.

5. Each of the five prayers is determined by the sun's position in the sky and your location. Source: https://www.pexels.com/photo/sunset-147465/

Fajr

Fajr is considered a blessed time. Although some struggle with waking up to pray at dawn, it can leave you feeling energized and well-rested. Prophet Muhammed (PBUH) said about the fajr prayer, *"Whoever offers the Morning Prayer, he is under the protection of Allah, the Mighty and Sublime."* Praying fajr on time can save you from hell, protect you from the devil, strengthen your faith, and grant you paradise. Prophet Muhammed (PBUH) said the two fajr rak'ahs are better than the world and everything in it.

Dhuhr

Dhuhr takes place at midday when Muslims are busy working or taking care of their chores. It is a reminder that nothing and no one is more significant than Allah (SWT). No matter how hectic your life gets, you should step back from the world to focus on your spiritual side and connect with Allah (SWT). Praying dhuhr on time will protect you from hell, increase your blessings, and reduce stress because it gives you a break from your busy life.

Asr

Prophet Muhammed (PBUH) spoke of the importance of the fajr and asr prayer, *"He who performs Salat (prayers) before the rising of the sun and before its setting, will not enter the Hell."*

Allah (SWT) also said in the holy Quran, *"Maintain with care the [obligatory] prayers and [in particular] the middle prayer and stand before Allah, devoutly obedient."* Quran 2:238.

Muslims should pray Asr on time and not delay it to enter paradise and be protected from hell. Asr also takes place when people are busy. Allah (SWT) will be pleased with you when you prioritize your worship and leave anything you are doing to pray.

Maghrib

Maghrib is a time to express your gratitude to Allah (SWT) and ask for His forgiveness. Muslims who pray maghrib on time bask in Allah's (SWT) blessings, have success in life, and their duas will be accepted if Allah (SWT) wills.

Isha

Isha prayer takes place at the end of the day when people are tired or about to go to sleep. It can be hard for some people to pray on time, which is why Allah (SWT) offers great rewards to those who do. Prophet Muhammed (PBUH) said, *"Whoever attends Isha (prayer) in congregation, then he has (the reward as if he had) stood half of the night. And whoever prays Isha and Fajr in congregation, then he has (the reward as if he had) spend the entire night standing (in prayer)."*

Allah (SWT) will bestow his blessings upon you when you pray isha and offer dua. Praying isha before bed will provide you with peace of mind and undisturbed sleep.

Prayers were set at specific times for a reason. So don't delay salah, and always make dua for yourself and your loved ones.

Chapter 3: The Right Way to Prepare for Salah

What is your first thought when you hear the adhan? You probably want to run to your praying mat and stand before Allah (SWT). However, you should first prepare by cleansing your body, organizing the prayer space, and dressing modestly.

6. Physical cleansing is part of your spiritual hygiene. Source: https://www.pexels.com/photo/woman-washing-her-hands-with-soap-4031819/

This chapter provides step-by-step instructions for wudu, explains the significance of cleanliness and modesty in preparation for prayer, and how to create a conducive environment for prayer at home or in the mosque.

Purification (Wudu): Step-by-Step Guide for Performing Ablution

Muslims shouldn't pray before performing ablution or wudu. Prophet Muhammed (PBUH) said, *"No Salat is accepted without Wudu."* Wudu is a mandatory spiritual and physical ritual that involves washing and cleansing certain body parts to remove impurities. Prophet Muhammed (PBUH) showed Muslims how to perform wudu and they have been following his lead ever since.

Wudu purifies the soul, removes sins, helps you attain the Almighty's love, and illuminates your face on Judgment Day.

Types of Wudu

Water

This is the most common type of wudu where you cleanse yourself with water.

Tayammum

If water isn't available, cleanse your body with sand.

1. Say *bismillah*.

2. Place your palms on the ground.

3. Rub your hands together.

4. Rub your face with your hands.

Ghusl

Ghusl is showering, and it takes place after the menstrual cycle is done or after intercourse.

Learn to perform wudu and make sure to follow instructions and cleanse each body part in the same order.

Step 1: Set Intention or Niyyah

Calm your thoughts and only focus on the act of worship. Before performing wudu, make sure that your niyyah is sincere towards cleansing your body to purify it and pray to Allah (SWT). You can set an intention with your heart and mind or say out loud, *"I intend to perform Wudu, seeking nearness to Allah SWT."*

Step 2: Say Bismillah

After you prepare yourself mentally for the act of wudu, say *Bismillah*, meaning *"In the name of Allah."* You can say it to yourself or out loud.

Step 3: Wash Your Hands

You should wash your hands first. Rub both hands together and rinse under clean water three times. Make sure to wash every part of your hands to the wrist and between the fingers.

7. You should wash your hands first.

Step 4: Wash Your Mouth

Fill your right hand with water, rinse the inside of your mouth, and spit the water out. Do this three times. Make sure the water reaches the back of your tongue and your gums. It is okay to swallow a little of the water unless you are fasting.

Step 5: Clean Your Nostrils

Fill your right hand with water, take it up into your nostrils, and blow it out using your left hand. Do this three times. Avoid inhaling too much water, as it isn't safe.

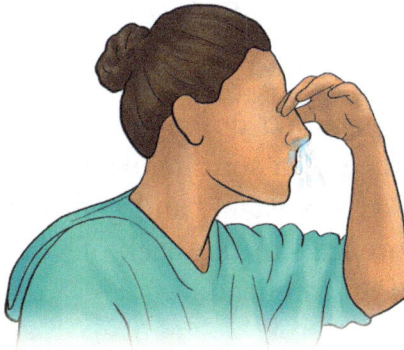

8. Cleaning nostrils.

Step 5: Wash Your Face

Fill your hands with water and wash your whole face, including the bottom of your chin, the top of your head, and the parts near the ears three times.

Step 6: Wash Your Arms

Start with the right arm and wash the fingertips up to the elbow three times then repeat with your left arm three times. Make sure the whole arm is wet, and no area is dry. Use enough water to clean your arms thoroughly.

9. *Wash the arms.*

Step 7: Wipe Your Head

In this step, you won't do any washing. You will simply wipe your head once. Wet your hands under the water, shake them to remove excess water, and gently move them from the top of the forehead to the back of your head and then back to the top of the forehead.

10. Wipe your head.

Step 8: Clean Your Ears

Clean your ears right after wiping your head without wetting your hands again. Put your thumbs behind your ears and your index finger inside and gently rub to remove wax or dirt. Clean both ears at the same time. Do this once.

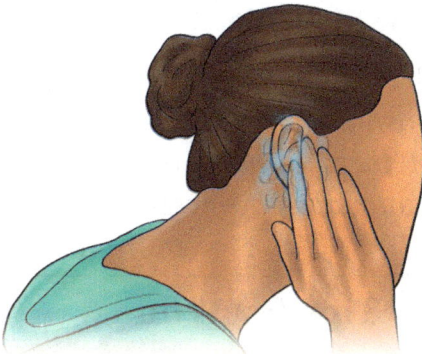

11. Wash your ears.

Step 9: Wash Your Feet

Your feet are the last to clean. Put your right foot under the running water and wash it. Begin at your toes and wash up until the ankle. Clean your foot with your right hand and between the toes with your finger. Do this three times and repeat with your left foot. Use enough water to cover the whole foot.

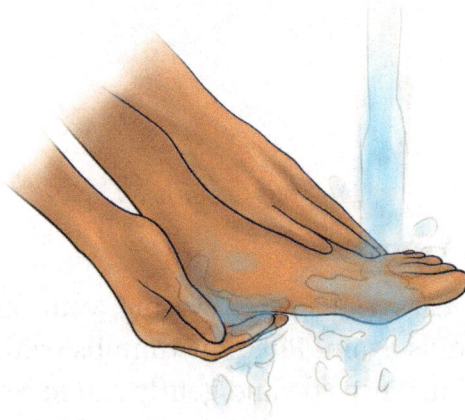

12. Wash your feet.

Step 10: Recite the Shahada

Recite the Shahada after you finish wudu, *"Ashhadu an la ilaha illAllah, wa ashhadu anna Muhammad rasulullah."* (I bear witness that there is no god but Allah, and I bear witness that Muhammad is the messenger of Allah).

Tips for Wudu

- Wudu should be done quickly. Don't wait before each step.
- Make sure every required body part is washed.

- Perform wudu in the correct order as shown above.

Importance of Cleanliness and Modesty in Preparation for Prayer

Prophet Muhammed (PBUH) said, *"Cleanliness is half of faith."* It is one of the most significant aspects of Islam and Salah. Your prayer won't be accepted without wudu. When Muslims perform wudu, they don't just wash their body. They purify it to cleanse impurities and sins. Wudu also purifies your soul so you are spiritually prepared to stand before Allah (SWT).

Wudu is an act of worship that protects you from sinning and temptation. Prophet Muhammed (PBUH) said, *"When a believer performs Wudu and washes his face, the angels cleanse his face, and every sin he has seen or committed with his eyes is washed away with the last drop of water. Then he washes his hands, the angels cleanse his hands, and every sin he has touched or committed with his hands is washed away with the last drop of water. After that, when he washes his feet, the angels cleanse his feet, and every sin he has walked to or committed with his feet is washed away with the last drop of water."*

If you have a meeting with your boss, how would you prepare for it? You would take a shower, brush your teeth, wear nice and clean clothes, etc. Now, imagine that this meeting is with Allah (SWT). Wouldn't you want to look your best?

Modesty is also important in preparation for prayer. Even if you pray alone at home, you should still dress modestly and cover your body to follow the teachings of Islam. One may argue that Allah (SWT) created all mankind and is aware of their bodies, so why should women cover up during salah?

When you pray to Allah (SWT), you should wear the appropriate clothing. For women, this involves wearing modest clothes that cover their bodies. Prophet Muhammed (PBUH) said, *"Allah does not accept the prayer of a woman who has reached puberty unless she wears a veil."*

Modesty begins in the heart. Before praying, remove your ego or the sense of entitlement from your heart. Humble yourself and remember who you are standing before. You may be a successful manager or one of the richest women in the world, but nothing can ever compare to Allah (SWT), the Creator of the universe.

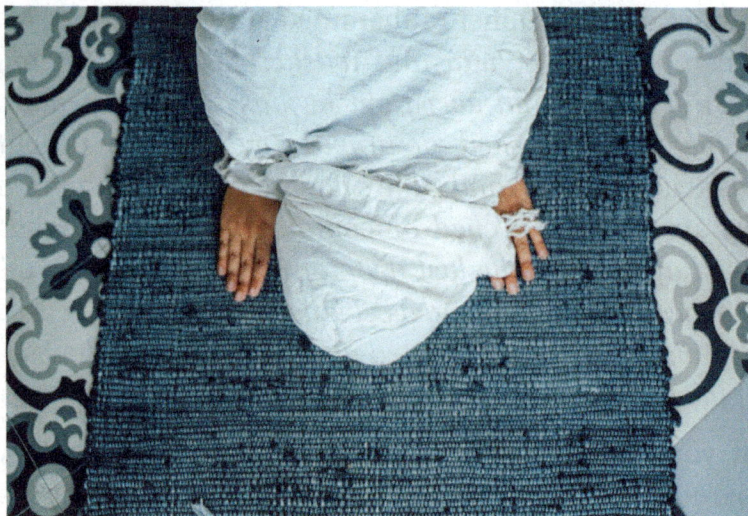

13. Modesty begins in the heart. Source:
https://www.pexels.com/photo/top-view-of-a-person-kneeling-8726484/

Creating a Conducive Environment for Prayer at Home or in the Mosque

You should assign a space in your home for salah. Remember that salah is a spiritual worship, and you need a peaceful environment to help you get into this frame of mind.

Qibla

Choose a room in your home where you can easily face the qibla. It can be a corner in your bedroom, living room, or any other room in the house. Make sure the space is big enough to fit a prayer mat and allows you to pray comfortably. Choosing a space by a window or corner facing a wall would be ideal. Eliminate all distractions from the room before praying. Turn off the TV or laptop, set your phone to silent, and tell the kids and other family members not to disturb you while praying. This space should only be for salah; don't use it for anything else.

The Color of the Walls

Avoid rooms with catchy wallpapers or bright colors, as they could distract you while praying. Choose rooms with calming or neutral colors.

Furniture

If you designate a whole room for salah, decorate it wisely. Don't add unnecessary furniture or items you won't use. Prayer mats, chairs for people who can't pray standing up, shelves for the Quran, and light spots are enough. Keep this in mind when organizing a paying space at a mosque.

Flooring

Cover the prayer room with a thick, soft carpet that will make you feel comfortable when you prostrate or sit on the floor. Unlike hardwood floors, carpets don't make noise when you walk on them, making them less distracting.

Adornments

Create an Islamic ambiance by decorating the room with Islamic artwork or verses from the Quran. Avoid any distracting adornments.

Make sure the room promotes a peaceful and calming atmosphere that allows you to connect with Allah (SWT) and enrich your spirituality.

Preparing for salah is as important as the prayer itself. Purify your body and soul by performing wudu. Stand before Allah (SWT) with modest and clean clothes. Designate a quiet room at home for salah and add simple decorations and furniture to avoid distractions.

Chapter 4: Step-by-Step Guide to Performing Salah

Salah is beautiful and simple. It involves a few physical movements and reciting verses from the Quran. Muslims should be focused when they perform the salah because they are in the presence of Allah (SWT) and must give Him their full attention.

14. Salah involves a few physical movements and reciting verses from the Quran. Source: https://www.pexels.com/photo/a-woman-in-traditional-dress-and-hijab-praying-7249366/

This chapter provides detailed instructions for each prayer, including physical movements, the recitation of surah al-Fatiha and additional Quranic verses in each rak'ah, guidance on maintaining proper focus and concentration during prayer, and tips on how to have a consistent prayer practice.

Detailed Instructions for Each Prayer

After performing wudu, dress modestly, place your praying mat on the floor in the direction of the qibla, and stand before Allah (SWT) and pray.

Step 1: Stand in the Direction of the Qibla

The qibla is in the direction of the Kaaba. Facing it is mandatory for your salah to be accepted. If you don't know the direction, you can download a qibla finder or a qibla compass app on your phone.

Step 2: Set an Intention

Set a niyyah before you start praying to prepare yourself spiritually for salah. You can either say it out loud or under your breath. Make an intention from the heart to leave the world behind and only focus on salah.

Step 3: Stand

Stand with both feet close together, open your fists, and raise your hands to shoulder level. Keep your gaze on the prostration space on the mat.

15. Raise your hands to shoulder level.

Step 4: Say Allahu Akbar

While your hands are still raised to shoulder level, say *"Allahu Akbar."* Now, you have started praying and should be completely focused on the act of salah. Don't allow anything or anyone to distract you.

16. Raised hands at shoulder level.

Step 5: Place Your Hands on Your Chest

Put your right palm over the back of your left hand and place them on your chest.

17. Place your hands on your chest.

Step 6: Say the Opening Supplication

Say the opening dua before reciting Al-Fatiha.

"Subḥānakal-lahumma wa biḥamdika wa tabārakas-muka wa taʿālā jadduka wa lā ilaha ghayruka."

"Glory to You, Oʾ Allah, with Your praise. Blessed is Your name, Exalted is Your Honor. There is no deity besides You."

Step 7: Recite Al-Fatiha

Begin by saying, *"Aʿūdhu biLlahi minash-shayṭānir-rajīm"* or *"I seek refuge in Allah from the accursed Shaytan (devil)."*

Next, say *"Bismillah ir Rahman ir Rahim"* or *"In the name of Allah, the infinitely Compassionate and Merciful."* Then recite Al-Fatiha.

Step 8: Recite Verses from the Quran

After reciting Al-Fatiha, recite a surah or any verses of your choice from the Quran.

Step 9: Bow Down

Bow down or perform ruku while saying *"Allahu Akbar."* Bend your back slightly without fully straightening it, and put both hands on your knees. Repeat *"Subhana Rabbiya al-Azeem"* or *"Glory be to my Lord Almighty"* three times. Keep your eyes on your feet.

18. Bow down or perform ruku while saying "Allahu Akbar.".

Step 10: Return to the Standing Position

Rise from the bowing position while placing your hands near your ears and say once, *"Sami'a Llahu liman ḥamidah"* or *"Allah hears those who praise him."* After returning to the standing position, lower your hands and say, *"Rabbana walak alhamd"* or *"Our Lord, to You is all praise."*

19. Rise from the bowing position while placing your hands near your ears.

Step 11: Prostration

Say *"Allahu Akbar"* and prostrate or perform sujud. Your toes, knees, palms, nose, and forehead should be touching the ground. Repeat three times, *"Subhana Rabbiyal A'la"* or *"How Perfect is my Lord, the Highest."* Sit up while saying, *"Allahu Akbar,"* and remain in this position for three seconds with your hands on your thigh and say *"Rab ighfir li"* or *"O my Lord! Forgive me,"* and return to the prostration position and repeat *"Subhana Rabbiyal A'la"* three times. Say, *"Allahu Akbar"* then return to the standing position.

20. Say "Allahu Akbar" and prostrate or perform sujud.

Step 12: Recite Tashahhud

You have now finished the first rak'ah. Repeat steps 7 to 11, and after you finish the second prostration of the second rak'ah, sit up, and recite the tashahhud.

"Attahiyat lillahi wa salawatu wa't-tayyibat, as-salamu 'alayka ayyuha'n-Nabiyyu wa rahmat-Allahi wa barakatuhu. As-salamu 'alayna wa 'alaa 'ibad-Illah is-saliheen. ashhadu alla ilaha illallah wa ashhadu anna muhammadan 'abduhu wa rasuluhu." Or *"All the best compliments and the prayers and the good things are for Allah. Peace and Allah's Mercy and Blessings be on you, O Prophet! Peace be on us and on the pious slaves of Allah, I testify that none has the right to be worshipped but Allah, and I also testify that Muhammad is Allah's slave and His Apostle."*

When you get to the shahada part in the tashahhud, make your hand into a fist and raise your index finger. This reflects the oneness of Allah (SWT).

After you finish the tashahhud, say *"Allahu Akbar,"* get back to the standing position, and continue praying until you get to the last rak'ah. After the last prostration, say the tashahhud then add the *"Salawat"* part.

"Allahumma salli 'ala Muhammadin Wa 'ala ali Muhammadin Kama sallaita 'ala Ibrahima wa 'ala ali Ibrahima wa barik 'ala Muhammadin wa 'ala ali Muhammadin Kama barakta ' ala Ibrahima Wa ' ala ali Ibrahima Fil a'lamina Innaka hamidun Majid." Or *"O Allah, let Your mercy come upon Muhammad and the family of Muhammad as You let it come upon Ibrahim and the family of Ibrahim O Allah, bless Muhammad and the family of Muhammad as You blessed Ibrahim and the family of Ibrahim. Truly You are Praiseworthy and Glorious."*

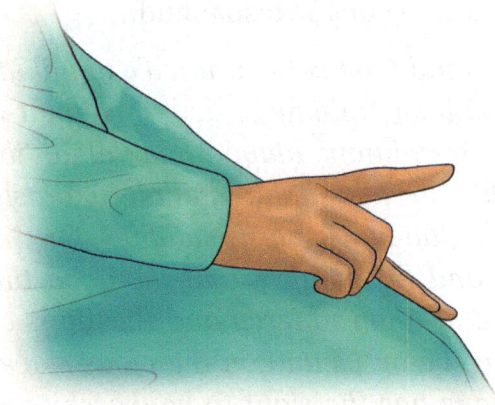

21. Make your hand into a fist and raise your index finger.

Step 13: Tasleem

After finishing the tashahhud and salawat, turn your face to the right and say *"Assalamu alaikum wa rahmatullah"* meaning, *"Peace and the mercy of Allah be on you."* Then, turn your face to the left and repeat the tasleem.

22. *Turn your face to the right and say, "Assalamu alaikum wa rahmatullah."*

Recitation of Surah Al-Fatiha and Additional Quranic verses (Surahs) in Each Rak'ah

You should first recite Al-Fatiha and then any Quranic verses in the first two rak'ahs. Only recite Al-Fatiha in any rak'ahs after the second.

"Alhamdu lillahi Rabbil 'aalameen Ar-Rahmaanir-Raheem Maaliki Yawmid-Deen Iyyaaka na'budu wa Iyyaaka nasta'een Ihdinas-Siraatal-Mustaqeem Siraatal-lazeena an'amta 'alaihim ghayril-maghdoobi 'alaihim wa lad-daaalleen." Then say *"Ameen."*

"Praise be to Allah, the Cherisher and Sustainer of the worlds; Most Gracious, Most Merciful; Master of the Day of Judgment. Thee do we worship, and Thine aid we seek. Show us the straight way, The way of those on whom Thou

hast bestowed Thy Grace, those whose (portion) is not wrath, and who go not astray."

Guidance on Maintaining Proper Focus and Concentration During Prayer

It is easy to get distracted while praying. If you have children and they play loudly, the sounds can affect your concentration. If you are preoccupied with something, such as a problem at work, these thoughts may creep in and distract you while praying. This can affect the spiritual connection you are trying to establish with Allah (SWT).

23. Remove any distractions during Salah. Source: Designed by Freepik. https://www.freepik.com/free-vector/audio-mute_37408831.htm

Follow these tips to improve your concentration:

- Pray in a quiet spot away from distractions.

- Dim the lights.

- Close the door and shut the windows to avoid outside noises.

- Put your cell phone on silent.

- Pray in an audible voice when you are alone. Hearing your own voice doesn't only help you concentrate but will also make you feel that you are talking to Allah (SWT).

- If you get distracted, remind yourself that you are standing before Allah (SWT).

- Sit for a few seconds after the second prostration in the first and third rak'ah where there is no tashahhud.

- Speak slowly and clearly while praying.

- No one can concentrate on something they don't understand. Learn the translation of the Quranic verses and supplications and focus on their meaning.

- Use different Quranic verses to avoid repetitiveness, which can affect your concentration.

- Make sure you are covered properly so you don't adjust your hijab while praying.

- Use the bathroom before praying and then perform wudu so you aren't distracted by relieving yourself.

- Don't rush in praying.

- Pray as if it is your last salah.

Tips for Maintaining a Consistent Prayer Practice

Some people pray for a few days or a week, then stop, or they only pray two or three prayers and ignore the rest. Salah isn't something to do in your free time, it is a priority and an essential part of your life. You should maintain a consistent prayer practice.

- Remind yourself of the significance of salah.

- Schedule everything around prayer time.

- Always perform wudu before you leave the house so you are prepared to pray anywhere.

- Don't delay salah and pray right after the adhan.

- Use an adhan app or a reminder so you don't forget to pray.

- Create a space for prayer.

- Ask Allah (SWT) to make salah the biggest part of your life.

- Remember why Muslims pray.

- Remember the spiritual benefits of salah.

- Make a conscious decision to commit to salah.

Although there are many steps to salah, it is actually simple and only takes you a few minutes to complete. Follow the salah instructions, and don't change movements. Memorize different Quranic verses and recite them in prayer to help you focus. Eliminate all noises and distractions that can affect your concentration. Always remind yourself that you are standing before Allah (SWT), and He is watching and listening to you.

Make salah an essential part of your life. It should always come first, and everything else comes next. If you struggle with concentration or committing to salah, ask Allah (SWT) to strengthen your relationship with Him and with all acts of worship.

Chapter 5: Women in Salah

Do you know that men and women perform salah differently? You have probably noticed that you cover your hair when praying while your brother, father or husband don't. However, they also perform some postures differently from women. Learning the difference between these will help you perform salah correctly.

24. Men and women have different roles during prayer. Source: https://www.pexels.com/photo/a-woman-kneeling-on-the-floor-8749777/

Some salah rules can be confusing to women. Should you pray after giving birth? Should you make up for the prayers you miss during menstruation?

This chapter explains the differences in prayer posture between men and women and the rules regarding menstruation and postnatal. You will also discover supplications for women's specific needs and concerns.

Differences in Prayer Postures Between Men and Women

Prophet Muhammed (PBUH) passed by two women praying and told them, *"When you prostrate, make part of your body touch the ground because a woman is unlike a man in these aspects."*

According to another narration, Prophet Muhammed (PBUH) said that women should put one thigh under the other when they sit. They should rest their stomachs over their thighs during prostration to avoid revealing any of their body parts. The blessed Prophet (PBUH) is pleased with women who offer prayer properly.

Men and women follow the same salah instructions and rules. The only differences are meant to keep their bodies concealed and protected.

Opening Takbir

During the opening Takbir (saying *Allahu Akbar*), women should raise their hands to their shoulders, while men should raise their hands to their ears. Women should also keep their hands under their sleeves to prevent their forearms from showing, while men can freely remove their hands.

25. Women should raise their hands to their shoulders.

Standing

When standing, women should put their right hands on their left ones and place them over their chests without clasping them. Men should clasp their hands together and put them under their navels.

26. Women should put their right hands on their left ones and place them over their chests.

Bowing

Women should bend their backs without fully straightening them, just enough to touch their knees. They also should keep their fingers closed, bend their knees, and place their palms on their knees without grasping them. Men should straighten their backs to align with their heads, spread their fingers, and straighten and grasp their knees.

27. *Women should bend their backs without fully straightening them.*

Prostration

During prostration, women should place their forearms on the floor while men should raise theirs above the ground. Women should rest their abdomens over their thighs, keep their upper arms at their sides, and rest their forearms on the ground. They should also bring their limbs together to remain modest. Men should keep their toes upright, while women shouldn't.

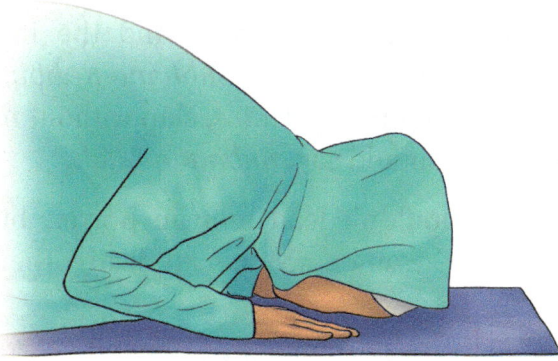

28. Women should place their forearms on the floor.

Sitting for Tashahhud

During tashahhud, women should rest their hands over their thighs, and their fingertips should reach their knees. Their fingers should be close together while men keep them apart.

29. During tashahhud, women should rest their hands over their thighs.

Other Differences

- If you pray in the mosque and the imam forgets something such as saying *Subhana Rabbiya al-Azeem* twice instead of three times, clap without moving your body. Men should say, *Subhana Allah.*

- Women shouldn't lead men in prayer, but they can lead other women. Men can lead other men and women.

- Women shouldn't call out the adhan or iqama.

- Women aren't obligated to attend Friday's prayer, unlike men.

Rulings Regarding Menstruation and Postnatal Bleeding

- Women experiencing menstrual or postnatal bleeding are prohibited from performing salah.

- After the bleeding stops, women must perform a ghusl to purify their bodies and perform acts of worship such as salah and fasting.

30. Shower to perform ghusl after the bleeding stops. Source: https://www.pexels.com/photo/black-shower-head-switched-on-161502/

- Performing ghusl involves washing both hands and arms, washing your private parts with your left hand, performing wudu, pouring water over your head three times, rubbing the hair with water, and washing your body, starting with your right side and then your left. Rub the water with your hands so it reaches every part of your body.

- You can make Takbir (saying *Allahu Akbar*), dhikr (remembering Allah (SWT), listen to the Quran, praise Allah, and read dua and hadith when you are menstruating or experiencing postnatal bleeding.

- Scholars have different opinions about women reading the Quran when they are menstruating. Some see nothing wrong with it, while others believe that women should only read the holy book with their hearts or eyes and avoid reciting it out loud. Many are inclined to follow the second opinion to be safe.

- They aren't allowed to fast, but they have to make up for the days they missed in Ramadan.

- They can fast when the bleeding stops and perform ghusl to purify their body.

- Menstruating women can perform all aspects of Umrah and Hajj except the tawaf or circumambulating the Kaaba.

- Some scholars say that menstruating and postnatal women are prohibited from entering the mosque, while others say that women can enter, provided they don't pray or read the Quran.

- Menstruating women are forbidden from having intercourse with their husbands.

- It is haram for a man to divorce his menstruating wife.

Supplications and Prayers for Women's Specific Needs and Concerns

Allah (SWT) has blessed Muslims with many supplications that they can use to pray for their needs or to ask to ease their concerns.

Duas for Anxiety and Depression

- *"La ilaha illa anta subhanaka inni kuntu minaz zalimin."*

   Translation: *"There is no god but You, exalted are You! Indeed, I have been of the wrongdoers."*

- *"Allahumma inni a'uzu bika min jahdil-bala', wa darki shaqa', wa su'il-qadha', wa shamatatil-a'da'."*

Translation: *"O Allah, I seek refuge in You from severe calamity, from misery to fall upon me, from misfortune in the decree, and from the joys of the enemies."*

- *"Rabbi-shrah li sodri, wa yassir li amri, wahlul uqdatan min lisani yafqohu qawli."*

Translation: *"Lord, lift up my heart and ease my task for me. Remove the impediment from my tongue so that they may understand my speech."*

- *"HasbiyAllahu la illaha illa Huwa, 'alayhi tawakkaltu, wa Huwa Rabbul arshil azim."*

Translation: *"Allah is sufficient for me. There is none worthy of worship but Him. I have placed my trust in Him, and He is the lord of the Majestic Throne."*

Dua to Protect from Sadness

"Allahumma inni a'udhu bika minal-hammi wal-Ḥuzni wal-'ajazi wal-kasli wal-bukhli wal-jubni wa ḍala'id-dayni wa ghalabatir-rijal."

Translation: *"O Allah, I take refuge in You from anxiety and sorrow, weakness and laziness, miserliness and cowardice, the burden of debts, and from being overpowered by men."*

31. Ask Allah (SWT) to protect you from the sadness that resides within your heart. Source: https://www.pexels.com/photo/photo-of-a-woman-praying-while-looking-up-7249241/

Dua When Distressed

"Allahumma rahmataka arju fala takilni ila nafsi tarfata 'aynin wa aslih li sha'ni kullahu la ilaha ila anta."

Translation: *"O Allah, I hope for Your mercy. Do not leave me to myself even for a blink of an eye. Correct all of my affairs for me. There is none worthy of worship except You."*

Dua for Attaining Confidence in Allah (SWT)

"Robbana, 'alaika tawakkalna, wa ilaika anabna, wa ilaikal-masir."

Translation: *"Our Lord! In You, we have placed our trust, and to You we turn in repentance, and to You is the final return."*

Dua to Protect from Illness

"Allāhumma innī a'ūdhu bika min al-baraṣi wa-al-junūni wa-al-judhāmi wa-min sayyi'i al-asqām."

Translation: *"Oh Allah! I seek refuge in you from vitiligo, madness, leprosy, and evil diseases."*

Dua for Protection

"Allāhumma innī as'aluka al-'āfiyah fī al-dunyá wa-al-ākhirah allāhumma innī as'aluka al-'afwah wa-al-'āfiyah fī dīnī wa-dunyāya wa-ahlī wa-mālī allāhumma ustur 'awrātī wa-āmin raw'ātī allāhumma iḥfaẓnī min bayni yadayya wa-min khalfī wa-'an yamīnī wa-'an shimālī wa-min fawqī wa-a'ūdhu bi-'aẓamatika an ughtāla min taḥtī."

Translation: *"O Allah, I ask You for well-being in this world and the Hereafter. O Allah, I ask You for pardon and well-being in my religion, my worldly affairs, my family, and my property. O Allah, conceal my faults and keep me safe from what I fear. O Allah, guard me from in front of me and behind me, on my right and on my left, and from above me. And I seek refuge in Your Magnificence from being swallowed up from beneath me."*

Dua to Ask Allah for a Child

"Rabbi hab lee mil ladunka d'urriyyatan t'ayyibah innaka samee-u'd du-a'aa."

Translation: *"My Lord, grant me from Yourself a good offspring. Indeed, You are the Hearer of supplication."*

Dua for Forgiveness

"Allahumma anta Rabbi, la ilaha illa anta, khalaqtani wa ana abduka, wa ana ala ahdika wa wa'dika mastata'tu, a'udhu bika min sharri ma sana'tu, aboo'u laka bini'matika alayya, wa aboo'u bithanbi faghfirli, fa innahu la yaghfiru althunooba illa anta."

Translation: *"O Allah, You are my Lord, there is no deity but You. You created me, and I am Your servant, and I abide by Your covenant and promise as best as I can. I seek refuge in You from the evil of what I have done. I acknowledge Your favor upon me, and I acknowledge my sin, so forgive me, for indeed none forgives sins except You."*

Duas for Your Children

- *"Rabbana hab lana min azwajinaa wa zurriyyatina qurrata a'yunin waj-alnaa lil muttaqiina imaama."*

    Translation: *"Our Lord! Bless us with pious spouses and offspring who will be the joy of our hearts, and make us models for the righteous."*

- *"Rabbij-'alni muqimas-solati wa min zurriyyati, Rabbana wa taqabbal du'a."*

    Translation: *"My Lord, make me an establisher of prayer, and from my descendants. Our Lord, and accept my supplication."*

Dua for Confidence

"Rabbi IshraH lee Sadree, wa yassirli amri, waHlul Uqdatan min lisani, yafqahu qawli."

Translation: *"Oh lord, expand my chest, ease my affair, and untie the knot in my tongue and perfect my expression."*

Dua When Feeling Lonely

"Allahumma Rahmataka Arju. Falaa takilnee ilaa nafsee Tarfata 'Ayn. Wa AsliH li Sha'ni kullahu, laa ilaaha illa anta."

Translation: *"O Allah, it is Your mercy that I hope for, so do not leave me in charge of my affairs even for a blink of an eye, and rectify for me all of my affairs. None has the right to be worshiped except You."*

Dua Before an Exam or Interview

"Rabbi-isyrahli sadri, wa yassir li amri, wahlul 'uqdatam-min lisaani yafqahu qawli."

Translations: *"My Lord! Uplift my heart for me, and ease for me my task. And remove the impediment from my tongue, so that they may understand my speech."*

Allah (SWT) is always there for you, listening to your prayers. Say what is in your heart, and He will ease your pain.

Chapter 6: Enhancing Your Salah Experience

Salah should be your main priority. It isn't something to do in your free time or put off when busy. Allah (SWT) calls on you five times a day. What can be more important than answering Him?

32. Salah should be your main priority. Source: https://www.pexels.com/photo/woman-kneeling-while-praying-8726453/

Life can be busy and filled with distractions, which can prevent you from connecting with your spiritual side. You may also struggle with praying regularly and devotion. However, Allah (SWT) will be pleased with you, and you will gain His blessings and rewards when you prioritize salah and are completely focused and devoted to the acts of worship.

This chapter explains the importance of regular praying and consistency in worship. You will also learn to improve your devotion and incorporate supplications in your daily prayer.

Importance of Regular Prayer and Consistency in Worship

Muslims pray to worship Allah (SWT) and to experience the beauty of connecting with Him and their spiritual side. Inconsistency in prayer deprives you of being close to Allah (SWT), worshiping Him, talking to him when you are sad, performing dua, and asking for His blessings.

Salah isn't a ritualistic practice or a chore that you complete and move on to something else. It involves unique moments and feelings that you won't experience anywhere else, such as supplication, spiritual reflection, and complete submission to Allah (SWT) and His will.

Regular prayer reminds you of your life purpose and why Allah (SWT) created you which is to serve and worship Him. Prophet Muhammed (PBUH) said, *"The most beloved deed to Allah is the most regular and constant even if it were little."*

Improves Your Spiritual Awareness

Performing salah regularly improves your spiritual awareness. It keeps you focused on and connected to your spiritual side and prevents you from being preoccupied with worldly matters. The lives of Muslims with high spiritual awareness are aligned with their beliefs and religion.

Close Relationship

The five prayers can lead to a personal and close relationship with the Almighty (SWT), but only if you pray every day and on time. Muslims can strengthen and nurture their relationship with Allah (SWT) through sincere and consistent worship.

Connecting with Allah (SWT)

Regular salah gives you a sense of belonging. No matter what happens to you or where you are, you know that Allah (SWT) is always with you, and you can turn to Him any time you want.

Resilience

Praying every day offers you a refuge from life's daily stresses and struggles. It provides reassurance and hope during your darkest times. You know that you will overcome whatever life throws your way because worshiping Allah (SWT) gives you strength. Salah empowers you and gives you resilience in the face of adversity.

Allah (SWT) said, *"Those who have believed and whose hearts are assured by the remembrance of Allah. Unquestionably, by the remembrance of Allah, hearts are assured."* Quran 13:28.

Spiritual Growth

Regular prayer strengthens your spiritual discipline. Repeating supplications and Quranic verses provides spiritual enlightenment and growth.

Inner Peace

Nothing can give you inner peace more than connecting with Allah (SWT). Reciting the Quran, inner reflection, and performing salah's rhythmic movement can give you peace of mind and provide you an escape from the chaos around you.

Tips for Improving Khushu (Devotion) in Salah

Khushu or devotion is the humility a person feels when they stand before Allah (SWT) during salah. It prevents your thoughts from wandering off and allows you to be more subdued, focused, and present. People with khushu in their hearts don't perform salah in a hurry but take their time and feel calm and at peace when praying. Khushu isn't obligatory in salah but is recommended. You will also gain many rewards from Allah (SWT) if you pray with devotion.

33. Take your time when you're praying. Source:
https://www.pexels.com/photo/a-woman-in-traditional-wear-sitting-on-a-prayer-rug-7249298/

Allah (SWT) said in the Quran, *"Successful indeed are the believers those who humble themselves in prayer."* Quran 23-1 and 23-2.

If you struggle with khushu, you can develop and improve it with these tips.

- You should truly know Allah (SWT)to become a better believer and Muslim. This will increase your love and faith in Him, which will impact your devotion.

- Stay away from sins and deeds that could anger Allah (SWT). This will purify your heart and open it up to receive and accept supplication and Quranic verses during salah.

- Read the Quran every day to soften your heart. A hard heart is unable to feel khushu.

- Focus more on your spiritual side and the afterlife while distancing yourself from worldly matters.

- Repeat after the muezzin when you hear the adhan. Stop everything you are doing and perform wudu to pray on time.

- Prepare yourself mentally for salah by taking a moment to think of this act of worship and who you are about to stand before.

- The moment you step on the praying mat, you are between Allah's (SWT) hands. Take in this feeling.

- Treat every salah as if it's your last one. Pray as if you will never get this chance again.

- Recite the Quran slowly and reflect on every word.

- Muslims are closest to Allah (SWT) during prostration to make supplications and ask him for His blessings and forgiveness.

- Ask Allah (SWT) to grant you khushu.

Incorporating Du'a (Supplication) and Dhikr (Remembrance of Allah) into Daily Prayers

Remembering Allah (SWT) should be a habit and a part of your daily routine. These tips will help incorporate dua into your daily life.

Repeat Dua Before Wudu

Say *"Bismillah"* before wudu to remember Allah (SWT) and prepare yourself mentally for salah.

Repeat Dua After Wudu

- *"Ash-hadu Anna La ilaaha illa Allah, wa Ash-hadu Anna Muhammed Aabdu-hu wa Rasulo-hu Allahuma ij'alni Mina attawabeen wa ij'alni mina al-mutatahiren."*

    Translation: *"I bear witness that there is no God but Allah, and I bear witness that Muhammad is his servant and messenger."*

- *"Subhan-aka Allah-ma wa Bi-Hamdik, Ash-hadu Anna La illaha illa anta, Astaghfir-uka wa atoubo ilik."*

    Translation: *"Glorified and praised are you, Allah. I bear witness there is no God except you. I ask for your forgiveness and repent to you."*

Say Dua Before Salah

- *"Subhanaka Allahumma wa bihamdika wa tabarakasmuka, wa ta'ala jadduka wa la ilaha ghairuk."*

    Translation: *"Glorious You are O Allah, and with Your praise, and blessed is Your Name, and exalted is Your majesty, and none has the right to be worshiped but You."*

- *"Allahumma, baa`id baini wa baina khatayaya kama baa`adta baina l-mashriqi wa l-maghrib. Allahumma, naqqini min khatayaya kama yunaqqa th-thawbu l-abyadu mina d-danas. Allahumma, ighsil khatayaya bi l-maa'i wa th-thalji wa l-barad."*

    Translation: *"O Allah! Set me apart from my sins (faults) as the East and West are set apart from each other and clean me from sins as a white garment is cleaned of dirt (after thorough washing). O Allah! Wash off my sins with water, snow, and hail."*

Say Dua After Salah

- *"La illaha ilal laahu wahdahu laa sharikalahu, lahul mul-ku, wala-hul hamdu, wahuwa alaa kuli shey'inn qadiir."*

    Translation: *"There is no god but Allah alone, He has no partners, to Him belongs dominion and to Him belongs praises, and He has power over all things."*

- *"Allahumma anta salaam, WA minka salaam, tabarakta yaa dhal jalali wal ikraaam."*

Translation: *"O Allah, you are the source of peace, and from you comes peace, exalted you are, o lord of majesty and honor."*

- *"Allahumma a'inni 'Aladhikrika, WA shukrika, WA husna iba datik."*

  Translation: *"O Allah, help me in remembering You, thanking You, and conducting my worship to You in a perfect way."*

- *"Astaghfirullāh [three times] Allāhumma antas-salām. wa minkas-salām. tabārakta yā dhal-Jalāli wal-'Ikrām."*

  Translation:*" *I seek the forgiveness of Allah (three times). O Allah, You are Peace, and from You comes peace. Blessed are You, O Owner of majesty and honor."*

- *"Lā 'ilāha 'illallāh. waḥdahu lā sharīka lah. lahul-mulku, wa lahul-ḥamd. wa huwa `alā kulli shay'in qadīr. Lā ḥawla wa lā quwwata 'illā billāh. lā 'ilāha 'illallāh. wa lā na`budu 'illā 'iyyāh. lahun-ni`matu wa lahul-faḍl. wa lahuth-thanā'ul-ḥasan. lā 'ilāha 'illallāh. mukhliṣīna lahud-dīn. wa law karihal-kāfirūn."*

  Translation: *"None has the right to be worshiped but Allah alone, He has no partner, His is the dominion and His is the praise and He is Able to do all things. There is no power and no might except by Allah. None has the right to be worshiped but Allah and we do not worship any other besides Him. His is grace, and His is bounty, and to Him belongs the most excellent praise. None has the right to be worshiped but Allah. (We are) sincere in making our* religious devotion to Him, even though the disbelievers may dislike it."

Recite Dua After Fajr and Maghrib

- "Lā 'ilāha 'illallāh. waḥdahu lā sharīka lah. lahu 'l-mulku wa lahu 'l-ḥamd. wa huwa `alā kulli shay'in qadīr."

  Translation: "None has the right to be worshiped but Allah alone, He has no partner, His is the dominion and His is the praise, and He is Able to do all things. O Allah, there is none who can withhold what You give, and none may give what You have withheld, and the might of the mighty person cannot benefit him against You." Repeat after the Maghrib prayer.

- "Allāhumma innī as'aluka `ilman nāfi`a, wa rizqan ṭayyiba, wa `amalan mutaqabbala."

  Translation: "O Allah, I ask You for knowledge which is beneficial, and sustenance which is good, and deeds which are acceptable." Repeat after fajr prayer.

- "Allahumma A jirny mina Annar." Translation: "O Allah, save me from the fire (Jahannam)."

Read Day and Evening Adhkar

Read morning and evening Adhkar every day. Download Hisnul Muslim app on your phone and set a reminder so you won't forget them. This app also contains many Adhkar recites for every occasion.

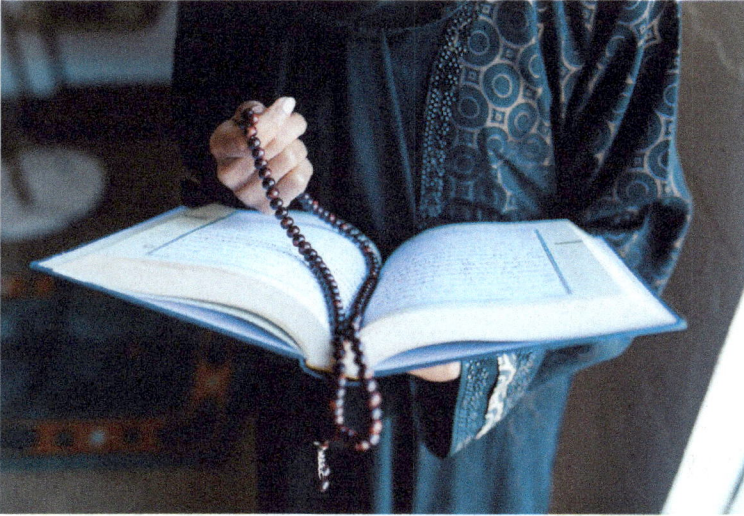

34. Read morning and evening Adhkar every day. Source: https://www.pexels.com/photo/crop-photo-of-woman-holding-a-prayer-beads-and-holy-book-7249191/

Incorporate duas into your daily routine by making time to recite them every day. You can also try to memorize them to repeat them at any time.

You should always recite Adhkar and remember Allah (SWT). This will soften your heart and protect you from sins. Those who have the Almighty (SWT) on their minds think twice before committing bad deeds that could anger Him.

Chapter 7: Overcoming Common Misconceptions and Challenges About Salah

Some people believe that no matter how hard they try, they will never be able to concentrate on salah. The human mind always wanders off, and you can easily get distracted while praying. For instance, if you have a big exam or job interview coming up, you may be preoccupied with it. However, this is what the shaitan or devil wants you to think. You can overcome salah challenges and pray with khushu.

35. You can overcome salah challenges and pray with khushu.
Source: https://www.pexels.com/photo/women-in-hijab-praying-7249339/

This chapter addresses the distractions and lack of focus during salah. It provides tips to deal with time constraints and busy schedules to find opportunities for salah and seek support and guidance from Islamic scholars. You will also learn about the common mistakes people make while praying.

Addressing Distractions and Lack of Focus During Salah

Shaitan wants to weaken your beliefs. He is constantly whispering in your ears to distract you from salah. Imagine you are praying and reciting Al-Fatiha. You are trying to concentrate when your thoughts begin to wander off to a dinner party you are hosting tomorrow. Will you have time to prepare everything? Will all your guests make it?

Suddenly you realize that you can't remember whether you have read verses after Al-Fatiha or not.

You feel guilty but think that focusing on salah is impossible. However, this is what the shaitan wants you to believe. Although maintaining concentration isn't always easy, you can achieve khushu and be completely focused on salah.

Think of all the times you lost focus while praying and find who or what distracted you and address the situation.

For instance, if your phone distracts you, put it in another room. If you have children and they play loudly, pray in a room alone and close the door. If you live in a loud neighborhood, shut the windows. If you usually have trouble concentrating, practice mindful meditation to help you stay focused on the present moment. Practice calming breathing exercises if you suffer from anxiety that makes your mind race or come up with scenarios that prevent you from focusing on salah.

You may do everything right but lose focus now and then. Don't be hard on yourself, you are a human and can have bad days. When your mind wanders off, bring your attention back to salah. Praying in an audible voice can also help you focus. You will be able to hear yourself reciting the Quran and dua, making it easier to connect with the words and their meaning.

The shaitan may make you think that Allah (SWT) won't accept your prayers when you are distracted. They may convince you to stop praying because the Almighty (SWT) isn't pleased with you. The devil can be so convincing, and you may listen to him.

Allah (SWT) is the most merciful and the most forgiving. He said in His holy book, *"Indeed, `it is` We `Who` created humankind and `fully` know what their souls whisper to them, and We are closer to them than `their` jugular vein."* Quran 50:16.

He is aware of what's in your heart and knows that you aren't doing this on purpose. However, this doesn't mean that you shouldn't try to overcome the distractions. Repent, ask Allah (SWT) for forgiveness, and try to improve your concentration. Allah (SWT) will be pleased with your efforts and how hard you work on yourself.

Keep in mind that distraction during salah is a sign that the devil is whispering to you. Prophet Muhammed (PBUH) said, *"When the call for prayer is made, Satan takes to his heels passing wind so that he may not hear the Adhan and when the call is finished he comes back, and when the Iqama is pronounced, Satan again takes to his heels, and when the Iqama is finished he comes back again and tries to interfere with the person and his thoughts and say, "Remember this and that (which he has not thought of before the prayer)", till the praying person forgets how much he has prayed. If anyone of you does not remember whether he has offered three or four rak`at then he should perform two prostrations of Sahu while sitting."*

Dealing with Time Constraints and Finding Opportunities for Prayer in Busy Schedules

Many women struggle to find a balance between their family, work, and faith. A working mother with two children may feel she doesn't have a minute for herself. Some days, you may feel overwhelmed and forget to pray or miss a salah and pray it later. Wudu and salah only take a few minutes, and no matter how busy you get, you can spare 10 or 15 minutes for Allah (SWT).

Use an Adhan app to remind you of your daily prayer, even on your busiest days. Once you get the notification, leave anything you are doing, perform wudu, and pray. If you are a teacher, doctor, or surgeon, you may not be able to pray right away. However, you can plan your day around salah. For instance, if you are a doctor, don't plan any appointments during praying time.

36. Set reminders on your phone to maintain prayer consistency. Source: Designed by Freepik.https://www.freepik.com/free-photo/muslim-woman-wearing-pink-sweater_11265319.htm

If you are in an important meeting, pray right after you finish. If your boss constantly watches over your shoulder, take a bathroom or lunch break, perform wudu, and pray. You can also incorporate salah into your schedule. While preparing your day or week, set ten minutes for each prayer. Adding a prayer to your schedule prioritizes it and gives a sense of urgency.

Remind yourself of Allah's many blessings on you and all the times you prayed to Him, and He gave you more than what you asked. This will encourage you to make time for salah even on your busiest days.

Seeking Support and Guidance from Knowledgeable Mentors or Scholars

Never stop learning. Islam is a beautiful and rich religion filled with stories that can enrich your life and teach you to be a better person. However, you may struggle with understanding certain rules and aspects of the religion or fail to understand certain verses from the Quran.

Seeking the support and guidance of a knowledgeable mentor and scholar can help you navigate the religion's complex parts, answer your questions, and ease your concerns. New converts may find some of the religion's rules confusing. For instance, they may not understand why nose drops break one's fast while brushing teeth is permitted. They may struggle to understand the importance of salah or other pillars of Islam.

Visit any local mosque and speak to an imam or a Quran teacher and seek their knowledge and advice.

Common Mistakes to Avoid When Praying

Rushing

How can someone be in a hurry when they are standing before Allah (SWT)? Unfortunately, some people treat salah as a race and rush through it. Rushing through salah will prevent you from concentrating, achieving khushu, and connecting with your spiritual side. Whatever task or chore is waiting for you can't be more important than worshiping Allah (SWT).

Looking Around While Praying

You should stand still while praying and focus your eyes on the place where you prostrate. Don't move your head, body, or eyes.

Wearing the Wrong Clothes

Some women think if they pray alone, they don't need to dress appropriately. They may wear tight clothes or a veil that doesn't cover all their hair. Prophet Muhammed (PBUH) instructed Muslim women to cover their awrah and avoid wearing tight clothes.

The Lack of Khushu

The lack of khushu is one of the most common mistakes people make in salah. Their mind is somewhere else, and they repeat Quranic verses and dua mindlessly without thinking about their meaning.

Incomplete Wudu

Muslims should perform wudu correctly and clean all the body parts recommended either one or three times. You can't wash your face twice or ignore cleaning your ears. Allah (SWT) may not accept your wudu or prayer.

Not Praying on Time

Allah (SWT) set a specific time for each prayer. Delaying salah shows that you don't prioritize worship and may reduce your reward.

Incorrect Recitation

Mispronouncing words or reciting the wrong verses can affect the salah's validity. Pray in an audible voice so you can hear yourself and correct any mistakes you make while praying.

Incorrect Movements

Salah involves performing certain movements that should be done as Prophet Muhammed (PBUH) instructed. You can't prostrate once or bow incorrectly.

Treating Salah as a Chore

You should pray with sincerity and humility. Don't perform your movements mechanically or recite the words without connecting with them. Always remember why you are praying and to whom.

The devil doesn't want you to focus on salah. He will distract you or prevent you from praying on time. Don't let him win. Resist these thoughts. Remember that you always have time to pray. No matter how busy your schedule is, you can find a few minutes to connect with the Almighty (SWT).

Make salah a priority and include it in your schedule. If you keep thinking that you don't have time, this is the devil trying to bring you down. You are stronger than him and won't let him control your thoughts or get between you and Allah (SWT).

Chapter 8: Frequently Asked Questions

Do you still have questions about salah? You will find all the answers you are seeking and more in this chapter. It also provides resources to help you learn more about praying and Islam.

37. Praying in the house has a bigger reward than praying in the house for women. Source: https://www.pexels.com/photo/women-in-hijab-sitting-on-floor-7249340/

Common Inquiries about Women in Islamic Prayer

1. Are Jumuah and Eid prayers mandatory for women?

No, the Jumuah and Eid prayers are mandatory for men, not women. Prophet Muhammed (PBUH) said, "The Friday prayer in congregation is a necessary duty for every Muslim, with four exceptions: a slave, a woman, a boy, and a sick person."

2. Do men and women have the same awrah?

No, men and women have different awrahs. Women must cover their whole bodies while praying except their hands and face. Men's awrah is the area between the naval and the knee.

3. Should women pray at home or in a mosque?

Prophet Muhammed (PBUH) said that women should pray at home and that their reward is bigger than praying in a mosque.

4. Is a woman's salah invalidated if a non-mahram saw her praying?

No, a woman's salah isn't invalidated if a non-mahram saw her pray. However, women should pray alone or with other women away from the prying eyes of strange men. This is why Prophet Muhammed (PBUH) preferred that women pray at home.

5. Can men and women pray together in Islam?

Yes, men and women can pray together, but they should stand behind men or be separated by a barrier.

6. Can you pray in English?

Yes, you can pray in English if you struggle with understanding Arabic.

7. When should you pray the missed salah?

A missed salah is one you haven't prayed on time and missed. If you forgot a salah or were asleep, pray it when you wake up or when you remember it. Missing a salah for no good reason is a sin. Repent to the Almighty (SWT), ask for His forgiveness, and promise not to miss a salah on purpose again. Pray the missed prayer with the current one. For instance, you forgot to pray el asr yesterday. Pray it with today's asr prayer.

8. What are the rewards of performing salah regularly?

It raises your rank in the afterlife, shields you from sin, grants you success, and protects you from hell. Performing salah on time is the dearest act of worship to Allah (SWT).

9. Are women allowed to pray after intercourse?

No, women aren't allowed to pray after intercourse. They should perform ghusl and purify their bodies first.

10. Should women make up for the salah they missed when they were menstruating?

No, women shouldn't make up for the salah they missed when they were menstruating. However, they should make up for the days they didn't fast in Ramadan.

11. Can women pray with makeup on?

Yes, women can pray with makeup on, but they shouldn't wear makeup in front of non-mahram.

12. Can women perform wudu with nail polish on?

Yes, they can unless it is made of substances that prevent water from reaching the skin. In this case, you will have to remove it, or your wudu will be invalid.

13. What can break wudu?

Bodily discharges such as gas, urine, and feces, deep slumber, touching your private parts, loss of consciousness, consuming camel meat, blood discharge, and vomiting. Repeat your wudu if any of these events occurred. You don't need to perform ghusl.

Additional Resources for Further Learning and Support

- https://myislam.org/short-surahs/
- https://apps.apple.com/gb/app/namaz-app-learn-salah-prayer/id1447056625
- https://www.newmuslims.com/
- https://iera.ca/new-muslim/learning-the-prayer/
- https://backtojannah.com/islamic-directory/
- https://islamonline.net/en/home/
- https://www.islamweb.net/en/
- https://www.islamicity.org/
- https://www.teacheron.com/online-qur_an_and_islamic_prayers-tutors
- https://www.quranproject.org/Muslim-Prayer-App-9-p
- https://www.teachmeislamapp.com/

- https://www.mymasjid.ca/beginners-guide-learn-pray-salah/
- https://getsajdah.com/
- https://aicp.org/index.php/islamic-information/text/english/73-the-basics-of-the-muslim-s-prayer-learn-how-to-pray
- https://www.muslimacoaching.com/step-by-step-prayer-guide-for-muslim-women/
- https://www.therevertchannel.com/
- https://apps.apple.com/us/app/salat-namaz-muslim-prayer/id875280793
- https://www.quranfocus.com/knowledge/read-prayer-namaz-salah-for-women-girls
- https://www.mysalahmat.com/?srsltid=AfmBOopzJk Y7lLXiLYsFOoGrZ-LPjoBO54awebgHOCJEBkoeOWSMyYHl
- https://www.teacheron.com/online-salat-tutors
- https://bayanulquran-academy.com/how-to-pray-salah/
- https://www.rabata.org/
- https://mahadsunnah.com/
- https://academy.seekersguidance.org/
- https://quranoasis.com/5-best-websites-to-learn-islamic-studies-online/
- https://destinationksa.com/the-best-websites-for-learning-authentic-islamic-knowledge/
- https://free-islamic-course.org/

- https://learn-islam.org/
- https://mishkahu.com/students/useful-links/
- https://quran.com/en
- https://read.quranexplorer.com/1/1/7/Usmani/Mishari-Rashid/Hide/Tajweed-OFF
- https://www.quranflash.com/home?en
- http://www.quranexplorer.com/
- https://sunnah.com/
- https://hadithcollection.com/
- https://ahadith.co.uk/
- https://www.alim.org/quran/?gad_source=1&gclid=CjoKCQjw_sq2BhCUARIsAIVqmQtdpAd2vg9oklVzRnaYeVxSXvluOhkQO6V_xhjp_47_LH2Tq8f5PmsaAh-QEALw_wcB
- https://quranonline.net/
- https://riwaqalquran.com/blog/quran-reading-websites/
- https://previous.quran.com/
- https://recitequran.com/1:1
- https://yhst-141393581866279.stores.turbify.net/s1010-quran-and-tafseer-english.html
- http://www.englishtafsir.com/
- https://www.altafsir.com/index.asp
- https://quran.com/en/al-fatihah/1/tafsirs

- https://www.abuaminaelias.com/dailyhadithonline/
- https://www.alim.org/hadith/
- https://www.sujood.co/
- https://www.islamicreliefcanada.org/resources/duas-and-dhikr
- https://lifewithallah.com/dhikr-dua/
- https://www.duas.org/
- https://www.islamicfinder.org/duas/
- https://duas.com/
- https://www.duaandazkar.com/
- https://www.islamestic.com/i-am-feeling/
- https://www.sujood.co/#emotion=anticipation

Remain Consistent in Implementing the Teachings of Salah in Your Everyday Lives

Salah teaches you commitment, loyalty, patience, devotion, focus, simplicity, and preparation. It also softens your heart, helps you identify priorities, and protects you from sinning and bad deeds. Salah connects you to Allah (SWT) and strengthens your relationship with him and your spiritual side. Implement these teachings with your family, friends, and at work. Be loyal, devoted, and soften your heart with everyone in your life.

Don't stop learning about salah or Islam. The more information you gather, the more you will love this beautiful religion. Visit your local mosque and speak to Islamic mentors, ask them questions, and expand your knowledge.

Pray every day and make salah a part of your life. Soon, it will become like water or the air you breathe, you won't be able to live without it.

Conclusion

Life isn't always easy, and you may struggle and feel alone. You may forget that Allah (SWT) is near you when things get hard, but performing the salah every day will remind you that the Almighty (SWT) is closer to you than your family and friends. Pray and prostate to Him, and you will feel the comfort and security of having a close relationship with Allah (SWT).

The book began by explaining the power of salah and its role in Islam. It also offered a detailed guide for girls and women on performing salah correctly and tips to deepen your connection with Allah (SWT).

You learned detailed information about the five prayers and the importance of setting niyyah before each one. Words to recite before every salah were also included.

The story behind how Allah (SWT) commanded salah reflects His mercy and Prophet Muhammed's (PBUH) love for all Muslims. You also understood the benefits of each salah.

The wudu guide was detailed and offered clear instructions on how to cleanse yourself before salah. You learned about the significance of modesty and cleanliness and how to create an environment suitable for praying.

Learning how to pray is easy. You just need to follow the instructions in the book, and in time, you will memorize them, and they will come naturally to you. You discovered how to overcome distractions with helpful tips to improve your focus.

The difference between how men and women perform salah will help you pray correctly and remain modest.

Women should know how to approach salah and other worships while menstruating or experiencing postnatal bleeding. This information is necessary for understanding Islam.

Having khushu in Islam will improve your salah experience and bring you close to Allah (SWT). Following the tips provided here will bring you closer to Allah (SWT).

The book ended by clearing misconceptions about salah, providing tips on making time for praying, and answering questions Muslim women need to know.

Key Takeaways

- Salah is one of the most important worships in Islam.
- You can connect with Allah (SWT) through prayer.
- Muslims should set a niyyah before any worship act.
- Wudu is mandatory before each prayer.
- Salah movements are simple, and you will grow accustomed to them with practice.
- Women should follow certain rules during menstruation or postnatal bleeding.

- You can improve your devotion and your concentration in salah.

References

Abdulla, A. (2020, March 11). How To Do Wudu - Step By Step For Beginners (2021 Guide). My Islam. https://myislam.org/how-to-do-wudu/

Abdulla, A. (2020, March 23). Opening Dua For Salah (Dua Al Istiftah). My Islam. https://myislam.org/opening-dua-of-salah/

About Wudu - Questions on Wudu Answered. (n.d.). Www.dudleyindustries.com. https://www.dudleyindustries.com/news/about-wudu-questions-on-wudu-answered

Ackbarali, N. (2020, March 9). What are the differences between a man and woman's prayer? - Islamic Counseling & Coaching. Islamic Counseling & Coaching.https://www.muslimacoaching.com/differences-between-man-and-woman-prayer/

Ackbarali, N. (2021, May 6). Step-by-Step Prayer Guide For Muslim Women - Muslima Coaching.Muslima Coaching. https://www.muslimacoaching.com/step-by-step-prayer-guide-for-muslim-women/

Adil. (2024, July). Duas For Pregnancy: A Guide for Expectant Mothers - Islamic Dua | Your Duas Database. Islamic Dua | Your Duas Database. https://matwproject.org/duas/dua-for-pregnancy/

Admin. (2022, October 31). Khushu — The Essential Quality of Prayer. Islam Channel. https://islamchannel.tv/khushu-the-essential-quality-of-prayer

Al-Basyuni, S. (2024, February 24). What Is The Importance Of Salah (Prayer) In Islam (Quran And Hadith)? - Sahlah Academy. Sahlah Academy. https://sahlahacademy.net/importance-of-salah

Alkurdi, Z. (2022, January 24). 9 Practical Tips to Developing a Prayer Habit. Medium. https://medium.com/@zeenakurdi/9-practical-tips-to-developing-a-prayer-habit-8b613f42ccc9

Amanat, A. (2021, December 14). How to Concentrate in Salah? (Dos and Don'ts). Faith Consulting. https://faith.consulting/blog/how-concentrate-salah-dos-and-donts

Ashraf Elessawy. (2014, April 7). O Allah, save me from the fire. Daily Dua'a; Daily Dua'a. https://dailyduaa.com/2014/04/07/o-allah-save-me-from-the-fire/

Awais, A. (2020, July 19). How to Increase Concentration in Salah. Islam Explained. https://islamexplained.info/2020/07/19/increase-concentration-during-salah/

Bano, S. (2022, October 10). How to Design a Prayer Room at Home? The Halal Times. https://www.halaltimes.com/how-to-design-a-prayer-room-at-home/

Basyony, S. (2024, February 10). How To Pray Salah For Females? - Bayan Al Quran Academy. Bayan al Quran Academy. https://bayanulquran-academy.com/how-to-pray-salah/

Bharakda, A. (2022, February 8). 16 Practical Tips to Stay Focused During Prayer. The Muslim Vibe. https://themuslimvibe.com/faith-islam/17-practical-tips-to-stay-focused-during-prayer

Chapter 2 – How to Make Wudu, Step by Step. (2016, October 31). Masjid Ar-Rahmah | Mosque of Mercy. https://www.mymasjid.ca/beginners-guide-learn-pray-salah/chapter-2/

Chapter 4 - How to Pray Salah, Step by Step. (n.d.). Masjid Ar-Rahmah | Mosque of Mercy. https://www.mymasjid.ca/beginners-guide-learn-pray-salah/chapter-4/

Chapter 5 – The 5 Daily Salah. (2016, October 31). Masjid Ar-Rahmah | Mosque of Mercy. https://www.mymasjid.ca/beginners-guide-learn-pray-salah/chapter-5/

Chapter 7 – Common Mistakes in Salah. (2016, October 31). Masjid Ar-Rahmah | Mosque of Mercy. https://www.mymasjid.ca/beginners-guide-learn-pray-salah/chapter-7/

Charity Right. (2024, February 13). Salah Made Easy: A Ten-Step Guide for How to Pray Salah. Charity Right. https://www.charityright.org.uk/blog/post/salah-made-easy-a-ten-step-guide-for-how-to-pray-salah

Dhuhr Prayer: Its Significance, Time, and How To Perform. (2023, February 28). Arabian Tongue. https://www.arabiantongue.com/dhuhr-prayer/#The-Significance-of-Dhuhr-Prayer

Dos and Don'ts during Menstruation - Islam Question & Answer. (30 C.E., September). Islamqa.info. https://islamqa.info/en/answers/70438/dos-and-donts-during-menstruation

Du'a After Salam (8 du'as) - My Islam. (2023, June 14). My Islam. https://myislam.org/dua-after-salam/

Duas & Supplications | Islamic Relief Canada. (2023). Islamic Relief Canada. https://www.islamicreliefcanada.org/resources/duas-and-dhikr

Editorial Team. (2024, May 10). Finding Peace in Prayer: Islamic Insights for Deepening Connection With Salah - Tazkiyah. Tazkiyah - Islamic Personal Development. https://kharchoufa.com/en/finding-peace-in-prayer-islamic-insights-for-deepening-connection-with-salah

eggy. (2024, July 11). The Spiritual Benefits of Daily Prayers in Islam - GlobalSadaqah.com Blog. GlobalSadaqah.com Blog. https://blog.globalsadaqah.com/the-spiritual-benefits-of-daily-prayers-in-islam

Habeeba. (2013, August). When In Salaat: 8 Ways to Increase Focus During Prayer - Muslim Girl. Muslim Girl. https://muslimgirl.com/when-in-salaat/

How to Perform Tayammum - Islam Question & Answer. (2002, January 2). Islamqa.info. https://islamqa.info/en/answers/21074/how-to-perform-tayammum

How To Pray Salah - A New Muslim's Guide. (n.d.). My Islam. https://myislam.org/how-to-pray-salah/

Idaraalfurqan. (2023, October 9). How to Perform Wudu – Step by Step Guide | Medium. Medium; Medium. https://medium.com/@idaraalfurqan11/how-to-perform-wudu-step-by-step-guide-e93d90215fe3

Iftaa, A. (2024). Women Praying in Front of Non- Mahrams. Egypt's Dar Al-Ifta. https://www.dar-alifta.org/en/fatwa/details/7926/women-praying-in-front-of-non-mahrams

Islam Web English. (2020, March 25). Islamweb.net. https://www.islamweb.net/en/fatwa/415666/lacks-khushoo%E2%80%99-in-prayer

IslamicFinder. (2024). 7 Tips to Improve the Habit of Offering Daily Salah | IslamicFinder. IslamicFinder. https://www.islamicfinder.org/news/7-tips-to-improve-the-habit-of-offering-daily-salah/

ItGirlReads. (2023, September 11). Five Daily Blessings: A Guide to Consistent Prayer in Islam. Medium; Medium. https://medium.com/@ITtGirlReads/five-daily-blessings-a-guide-to-consistent-prayer-in-islam-5457e745b87

Jami` at-Tirmidhi 221 - The Book on Salat (Prayer) - كتاب الصلاة - Sunnah.com - Sayings and Teachings of Prophet Muhammad (صلى الله عليه و سلم). (2024). Sunnah.com. https://sunnah.com/tirmidhi:221

Khan, A. (2020, September 24). How to Offer Salah Five Times a Day with a Busy Schedule. Medium; Medium. https://medium.com/@awaiskhan1191/how-to-offer-salah-five-times-a-day-with-a-busy-schedule-1c749189a748

Maghrib Prayer: Its Significance, Time, and How To Perform. (2023, February 27). Arabian Tongue. https://www.arabiantongue.com/maghrib-prayer/#Significance-of-Maghrib-Prayer

Makarem Shirazi, N. (n.d.). Question 11: Why Should Women Cover Themselves In Prayers? Al-Islam. https://www.al-islam.org/philosophy-islamic-laws-naser-makarem-shirazi-jafar-subhani/question-11-why-should-women-cover

Malti, F. (2021, September 19). Duas for Distress: Allah's help in challenging times. Muslim Women Australia. https://mwa.org.au/latest-articles/duas-for-distress-allahs-help-in-challenging-times/

Muslim Hands. (2019, March 28). The Five Daily Prayer Times and Why We Observe Them | Muslim Hands UK. Muslimhands.org.uk. https://muslimhands.org.uk/latest/2019/03/the-five-daily-prayer-times-and-why-we-observe-them

Muslim.Sg. (2020a, July 12). Dua for Anxiety and Depression. Muslim.sg. https://muslim.sg/articles/dua-for-anxiety-and-depression

Muslim.Sg. (2020b, October 2). Dua for Success in Everything. Muslim.sg. https://muslim.sg/articles/dua-for-success-in-everything

Muslim.Sg. (2022, December 14). How to Perform Wudhu – A Step-by-Step Guide for Beginners. Muslim.sg. https://muslim.sg/articles/how-to-perform-wudhu-a-step-by-step-guide-for-beginners

Muslim.Sg. (2021, January 9). Duas For Children's Success, Protection, Behaviour, Obedience, Guidance, Good Health and Safety. Muslim.sg. https://muslim.sg/articles/duas-for-children-s-success-protection-behaviour-obedience-guidance-good-health-and-safety

Noor Ul Islam. (2024, March 5). Mistakes to Avoid During Worship - Noor Ul Islam. Noor Ul Islam. https://www.noorulislam.org.uk/mistakes-to-avoid-during-worship/

Prayer Guide Blog: The Importance and Benefits of Salah in Islam. (n.d.). Muslim Rose Welfare. https://www.muslimrosewelfare.org.uk/blog/prayer-guide-blog-the-importance-and-benefits-of-salah-in-islam

Principles of Fiqh. (2024). Islam Question & Answer. Islamqa.info. https://islamqa.info/en/answers/12612/a-woman-has-to-cover-her-body-when-praying-even-when-she-is-behind-her-husband

Quran Tafseer. (2024). Maintain with Care the [Obligatory] Prayers and [In Particular] the Middle Prayer | Surah Baqarah Aya 238.Surahquran.com. https://surahquran.com/english-aya-238-sora-2.html

Resala Academy. (2022, December 25). Ultimate Guide for Wudu. Resala Academy. https://resala-academy.com/wudu-steps/

Saber, R. (2023, October 7). What Breaks Wudu? The 7 Vital Factors Explained. Learn Quran Online, Arabic & Islamic Studies Online | IQRA Network. https://iqranetwork.com/blog/7-key-events-breaking-wudu-explained/

Sahih al-Bukhari 1231 - Forgetfulness in Prayer - كتاب السهو - Sunnah.com - Sayings and Teachings of Prophet Muhammad (2024) (صلى الله عليه و سلم). Sunnah.com. https://sunnah.com/bukhari:1231

Sahih al-Bukhari 6464 - To make the Heart Tender (Ar-Riqaq) - كتاب الرقاق - Sunnah.com - Sayings and Teachings of Prophet Muhammad (صلى الله عليه و سلم). (n.d.). Sunnah.com. https://sunnah.com/bukhari:6464

Salah Rules for Women. (n.d.). https://www.icorlando.org/pdfs/women-salah.pdf

Salah. (2014). Learn Islam. https://learn-islam.org/class-6-supplications-after-salah

Shahinda. (2024, May). What Is the Virtue of Fajr Prayer? | Studio Arabiya in Egypt. Studio Arabiya in Egypt. https://www.studioarabiyainegypt.com/what-is-the-virtue-of-fajr-prayer/

Sunan Abi Dawud 1067 - Prayer (Kitab Al-Salat) - كتاب الصلاة - Sunnah.com - Sayings and Teachings of Prophet Muhammad (صلى الله عليه و سلم). (n.d.). Sunnah.com. https://sunnah.com/abudawud:1067

Surah Al-Mu'minun - 1-2 - Quran.com. (2024). Quran.com. https://quran.com/en/al-muminun/1-2

Surah Ar-Ra'd Ayat 28 (13:28 Quran) With Tafsir. (n.d.). My Islam. https://myislam.org/surah-rad/ayat-28/

Surah Qaf - 16. (n.d.). Quran.com. https://quran.com/en/qaf/16

Surat Al-`Ankabut [29:45] - The Noble Qur'an - 2024) (القرآن الكريم. Quran.com. https://legacy.quran.com/29/45

Tabassum. (2023, March 17). Why Can't We Always Be Close to Allah? | About Islam. About Islam. https://aboutislam.net/spirituality/why-cant-we-always-be-close-to-allah/

The Adhan (The Call to Prayer). (2021, November 5). IslamOnline. https://islamonline.net/en/the-adhan-the-call-to-prayer/

The Book of Virtues - Sunnah.com - Sayings and Teachings of Prophet Muhammad (2024) (صلى الله عليه و سلم). Sunnah.com. https://sunnah.com/riyadussalihin/8

to. (2014, June 23). Is It Permissible to Pray After Intercourse? Islam Stack Exchange. https://islam.stackexchange.com/questions/14723/is-it-permissable-to-pray-after-intercourse

Various Scholars. (2013, December 31). How to Gain Khushu in Salah. Islamway.net; Islamway. https://en.islamway.net/article/20269/how-to-gain-khushu-in-salah

What is Salah (salat)? (n.d.). Islamic Relief. https://www.islamic-relief.org.uk/resources/knowledge-base/five-pillars-of-islam/salah/

What Is the `Awrah of a Man? - Islam Question & Answer. (2012, May 22). Islamqa.info. https://islamqa.info/en/answers/171584/what-is-the-awrah-of-a-man

Wudu Dua: Dua Before Wudu And After Wudu In Arabic, English, And Transliteration - Riwaq Al Quran. (2024, March 27). Riwaq al Quran. https://riwaqalquran.com/blog/wudu-dua/#Dua-before-Wudu

Wudu Steps: How To Perform Wudu? - Riwaq Al Quran. (2024, April 19). Riwaq al Quran. https://riwaqalquran.com/blog/wudu-steps/#Whats-Wudu

Yasin, S. (2023, November 24). Importance of Wudu and Its Benefits in Islam | AwwalQuran. Awwal Quran. https://awwalquran.com/importance-of-wudu/

Zahra, S., & super-mqblog. (2021, October 25). How to Perform Wudu – A Step-by-Step Guide for Beginners.Muslim and Quran; app-id=1508575206. https://blog.muslimandquran.com/how-to-perform-wudu-step-by-step-guide-for-beginners/

Zarairfan. (2018, December 7). Benefits and Blessings of 5 Times Prayers in Islam. Islamic Articles. https://www.quranreading.com/blog/benefits-and-blessings-of-5-times-prayers-in-islam/

Made in the USA
Las Vegas, NV
23 February 2025

18581713R00056